CHRISTMAS SONGS

22 SONGS WITH CHORDS, LYRICS & BASIC TAB

T0088578

ISBN 978-1-5400-5415-9

HAL•LEONARD®

Visit Hal Leonard Online at
www.halleonard.com

Contact us:
Hal Leonard
7777 West Bluemound Road
Milwaukee, WI 53213
Email: info@halleonard.com

In Europe, contact:
Hal Leonard Europe Limited
42 Wigmore Street
Marylebone, London, W1U 2RN
Email: info@halleonardeurope.com

In Australia, contact:
Hal Leonard Australia Pty. Ltd.
4 Lentara Court
Cheltenham, Victoria, 3192 Australia
Email: info@halleonard.com.au

All I Want for Christmas Is My Two Front Teeth

Words and Music by Don Gardner

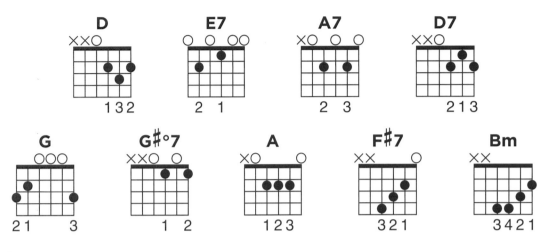

CHORUS 1

Moderately slow

D   E7   A7   D
All I want for Christmas is my two front teeth, my two front teeth, see, my two front teeth.

          E7   A7   D   D7
Gee, if I could only have my two front teeth, then I could wish you, "Merry Christmas!"

VERSE 1

 G   G#°7   D   A   D   F#7
It seems so long since I could say, "Sister Suzy sitting on a thistle."

Bm   E7 A7
Every time I try to speak, all I do is whistle.

CHORUS 2

D   E7   A7   D
All I want for Christmas is my two front teeth, my two front teeth, see, my two front teeth.

    D7   G   G#°7 D A7   D
Gee, if I could only have my two front teeth, then I could wish you, "Merry Christmas!"

VERSE 2

 G   G#°7   D   A   D F#7
 Good 'ol Santa Claus and all his reindeer, they used to bring me lots of toys and candy. Gee, but

Bm   E7   A7
now when I go out and call, "Dancer, Prancer, Donner and Blitzen," none of them can understand me.

CHORUS 3

D   E7   A7   D

All I want for Christmas is my two front teeth, my two front teeth, see, my two front teeth.

                 D7   G   G♯°7   D A7   D   N.C.

All I want for Christmas is my two front teeth, so I can wish you, "Merry Christmas!"

                                                            D

Christmas. Christmas. Oh, for goodness sakes! Happy New Year!

Blue Christmas

Words and Music by Billy Hayes and Jay Johnson

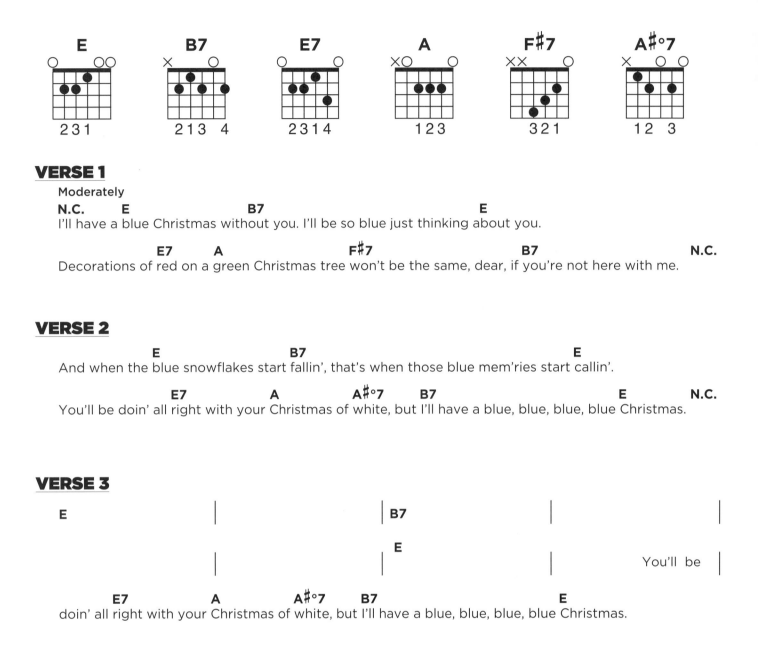

VERSE 1

Moderately

N.C.   E   B7   E
I'll have a blue Christmas without you. I'll be so blue just thinking about you.

    E7   A   F♯7   B7   N.C.
Decorations of red on a green Christmas tree won't be the same, dear, if you're not here with me.

VERSE 2

    E   B7   E
And when the blue snowflakes start fallin', that's when those blue mem'ries start callin'.

    E7   A   A♯°7 B7   E   N.C.
You'll be doin' all right with your Christmas of white, but I'll have a blue, blue, blue, blue Christmas.

VERSE 3

E | |B7 | |

     | |E | You'll be |

    E7   A   A♯°7 B7   E
doin' all right with your Christmas of white, but I'll have a blue, blue, blue, blue Christmas.

Christmas Time Is Here

from A CHARLIE BROWN CHRISTMAS

Words by Lee Mendelson
Music by Vince Guaraldi

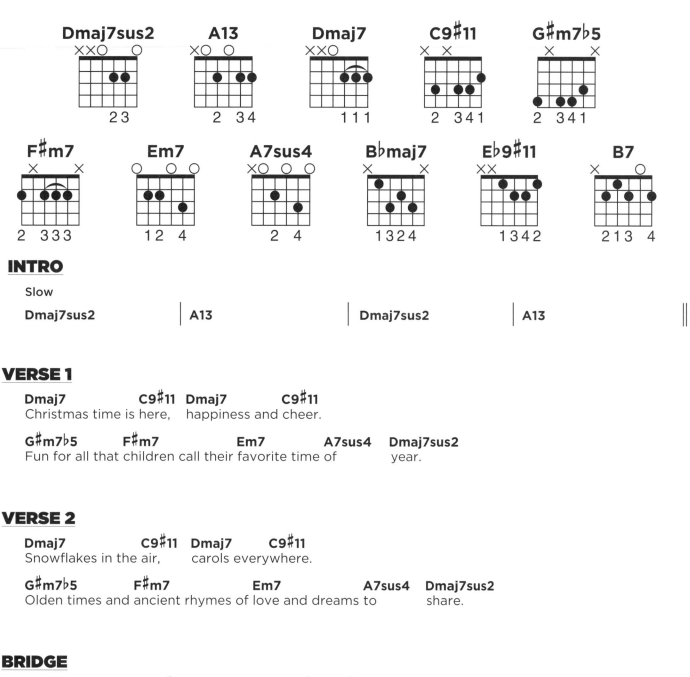

INTRO

Slow

Dmaj7sus2	A13		Dmaj7sus2	A13	

VERSE 1

Dmaj7   **C9#11** **Dmaj7**   **C9#11**
Christmas time is here,   happiness and cheer.

G#m7♭5   **F#m7**   **Em7**   **A7sus4**   **Dmaj7sus2**
Fun for all that children call their favorite time of   year.

VERSE 2

Dmaj7   **C9#11** **Dmaj7**   **C9#11**
Snowflakes in the air,   carols everywhere.

G#m7♭5   **F#m7**   **Em7**   **A7sus4**   **Dmaj7sus2**
Olden times and ancient rhymes of love and dreams to   share.

BRIDGE

B♭maj7   **E♭9#11** **B♭maj7**   **E♭9#11** **F#m7**   **B7**   **Em7**   **A13**
Sleigh-bells in the air,   beauty everywhere.   Yuletide by the fireside and joyful memories there.

VERSE 3

Dmaj7   **C9#11** **Dmaj7**   **C9#11**
Christmas time is here,   we'll be drawing near.

G#m7♭5   **F#m7**   **Em7**   **A7sus4**   **Dmaj7sus2**
Oh, that we could always see such spirit through the   year.

Do You Hear What I Hear

Words and Music by Noel Regney and Gloria Shayne

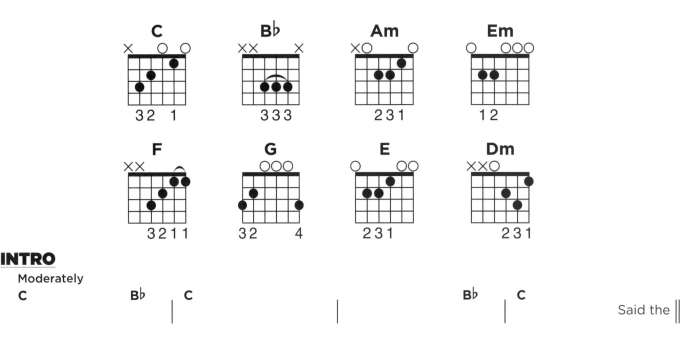

INTRO

Moderately

C   Bb   C   Bb   C

Said the

VERSE 1

C   Bb C
night wind to the little lamb, do you see what I see? (Do you see what I see?)

                       Bb C
Way up in the sky, little lamb, do you see what I see? (Do you see what I see?)

  Am   Em   F   G   E
A star, a star, dancing in the night, with a tail as big as a kite,

     F   G   C   Bb C
with a tail as big as a kite.

VERSE 2

          C   Bb   C
Said the little lamb to the shepherd boy, do you hear what I hear? (Do you hear what I hear?)

                 Bb   C
Ringing through the sky, shepherd boy, do you hear what I hear? (Do you hear what I hear?)

  Am   Em   F   G   E
A song, a song, high above the tree, with a voice as big as the sea,

     F   G   C   Bb C
with a voice as big as the sea.

VERSE 3

           C   B♭   C

Said the shepherd boy to the mighty king, do you know what I know? (Do you know what I know?)

                   B♭   C

In your palace warm, mighty king, do you know what I know? (Do you know what I know?)

  Am   Em   F   G   E

A Child, a Child shivers in the cold. Let us bring Him silver and gold.

     F   G   C   B♭ C

Let us bring Him silver and gold.

VERSE 4

           C   B♭   C

Said the king to the people everywhere, listen to what I say! (Listen to what I say!)

                   B♭   C

Pray for peace, people everywhere. Listen to what I say! (Listen to what I say!)

  Am   Em   F   G   E

The Child, the Child, sleeping in the night, He will bring us goodness and light.

     F   C Dm   G   C

He will bring us goodness   and light.

Feliz Navidad

Music and Lyrics by José Feliciano

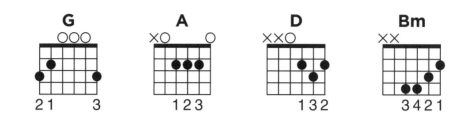

CHORUS

Moderately fast

|N.C.| |G|A| |D| |G| |A| |D|
Feliz Navidad, feliz Navidad, feliz Navidad, prospero a - ño y felicidad.

|N.C.| |G|A| |D| |G| |A| |D|
Feliz Navidad, feliz Navidad, feliz Navidad, prospero a - ño y felicidad.

VERSE

|N.C.| |G| |A| |D| |Bm|
I want to wish you a merry Christmas.   I want to wish you a merry Christmas.

|G| |A|D|
I want to wish you a merry Christmas from the bottom of my heart.

|N.C.| |G| |A| |D| |Bm|
I want to wish you a merry Christmas.   I want to wish you a merry Christmas.

|G| |A|D|
I want to wish you a merry Christmas from the bottom of my heart.

REPEAT CHORUS

REPEAT VERSE

OUTRO

|N.C.| |G|A| |D| |G| |A| |D|
Feliz Navidad, feliz Navidad, feliz Navidad, prospero a - ño y felicidad.

A Holly Jolly Christmas

Music and Lyrics by Johnny Marks

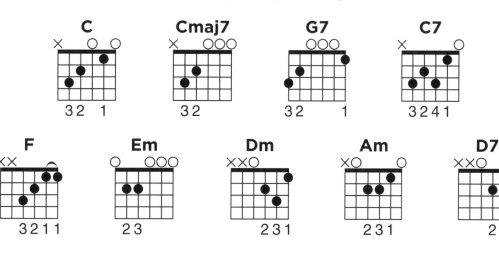

VERSE 1

Moderately fast

      C   **Cmaj7** **C**   **G7**
Have a holly jolly   Christmas, it's the best time of the year.

                                     C
I don't know if there'll be snow, but have a cup of cheer.

      Cmaj7 **C**   **G7**
Have a holly jolly   Christmas, and when you walk down the street,

                         C   **C7**
say hello to friends you know and everyone you meet.

BRIDGE

F   **Em**   **Dm**   **G7**   **C**
Oh, ho, the mistletoe hung where you can see.

Dm   **Am**   **D7**   **G7**
Somebody waits for you; kiss her once for me.

VERSE 2

C   **Cmaj7** **C**   **G7**
Have a holly jolly   Christmas, and in case you didn't hear,

             C   **D7**   **G7** **C**
oh, by golly, have a holly jolly Christmas   this year.

REPEAT VERSE 1

REPEAT BRIDGE

REPEAT VERSE 2

Frosty the Snow Man

Words and Music by Steve Nelson and Jack Rollins

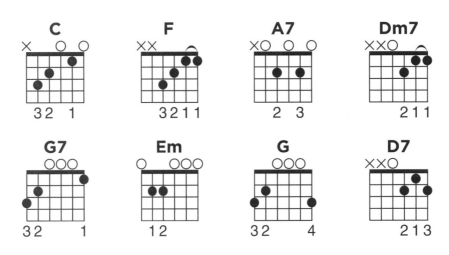

VERSE 1

Moderately slow

C   F   C
Frosty the snow man was a jolly, happy soul

      F   C   A7   Dm7   G7   C   G7
with a corn-cob pipe and a button nose and two eyes made out of coal.

C   F   C
Frosty the snow man is a fairy tale, they say.

      F   C   A7   Dm7   G7   C
He was made of snow, but the children know how he came to life one day.

BRIDGE 1

      F   Em   Dm7 G7   C
There must have been some magic in that old silk hat they found,

    G   D7   G7
for when they placed it on his head, he began to dance around.

VERSE 2

C   F   C
Frosty the snow man was alive as he could be,

     F   C   A7   Dm7 G7   C
and the children say he could laugh and play just the same as you and me.

VERSE 3

C   F   C
Frosty the snow man knew the sun was hot that day,

      F   C   A7   Dm7 G7   C   G7
so he said, "Let's run, and we'll have some fun now before I melt away."

C   F   C
Down to the village with a broomstick in his hand,

      F   C   A7   Dm7   G7   C
running here and there all around the square sayin', "Catch me if you can."

BRIDGE 2

      F   Em   Dm7 G7   C
He led them down the streets of town right to the traffic cop,

      G   D7   G7
and he only paused a moment when he heard him holler, "Stop!"

VERSE 4

      C   F   C
For Frosty the snow man had to hurry on his way,

      F   C   A7   Dm7 G7   C
but he waved goodbye sayin', "Don't you cry, I'll be back again someday."

OUTRO

C   G7
Thumpety, thump, thump, thumpety, thump, thump, look at Frosty go.

C   G7   C
Thumpety, thump, thump, thumpety, thump, thump, over the hills of snow.

Happy Xmas (War Is Over)

Written by John Lennon and Yoko Ono

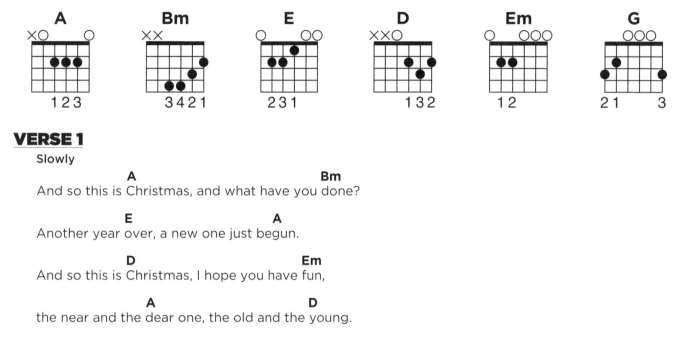

VERSE 1

Slowly

             A   **Bm**
And so this is Christmas, and what have you done?

             E   **A**
Another year over, a new one just begun.

             D   **Em**
And so this is Christmas, I hope you have fun,

             A   **D**
the near and the dear one, the old and the young.

CHORUS

             G   **A**
A very merry Christmas and a happy new year.

             Em   **G**   **D**   **E**
Let's hope it's a good one   without any fear.

VERSE 2

             A   **Bm**
And so this is Christmas, for weak and for strong,

             E   **A**
the rich and the poor ones, the road is so long.

             D   **Em**
And so, happy Christmas for black and for white,

             A   **D**
for yellow and red ones, let's stop all the fight.

REPEAT CHORUS

VERSE 3

              A   **Bm**
And so this is Christmas, and what have we done?

            E   **A**
Another year over, a new one just begun.

            D   **Em**
And so happy Christmas, we hope you have fun,

                 A   **D**
the near and the dear one, the old and the young.

REPEAT CHORUS

OUTRO

A   **Bm**   **E**   **A**
War is over if you want it. War is over now.

Have Yourself a Merry Little Christmas

from MEET ME IN ST. LOUIS

Words and Music by Hugh Martin and Ralph Blane

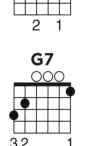

VERSE 1

Slowly

| G | | Em7 | Am7 | | D7 | | G | | Em7 | Am7 | | D7 |

Have yourself a merry little Christmas. Let your heart be light.

| G | | Em7 | Am7 | | D7 | B7 | | E7 | | A7 | | D7 |

From now on our troubles will be out of sight.

| G | | Em7 | Am7 | | D7 | | G | | Em7 | Am7 | | D7 |

Have yourself a merry little Christmas. Make the Yuletide gay.

| G | | Em7 | Am7 | | B7 | Em7 | | | | G7 |

From now on our troubles will be miles away.

BRIDGE

| Cmaj7 | Cm(maj7) | Bm7 | | Bb°7 | | Am7 | | D7 | Gmaj7 |

Here we are   as in olden days,   happy golden days   of yore.

| C#m7b5 | F#7b9 | | Bm7 | E7 | | D | | A7 | | D7 |

Faithful   friends who are dear to us   gather near to us   once more.

VERSE 2

G   Em7   Am7   D7   G   Em7 Am7   D7
Through the years we all will be together, if the fates allow.

G   Em7 Am7   B7   Em7   G7
Hang a shining star upon the highest bough,

   Cmaj7   Am7   D7   G   G7
and have yourself a merry little Christmas now.

REPEAT BRIDGE

VERSE 3

G   Em7   Am7   D7   G   Em7 Am7   D7
Through the years we all will be together, if the fates allow.

G   Em7 Am7   B7   Em7   G7
Hang a shining star upon the highest bough,

   Cmaj7   Am7   D7   G
and have yourself a merry little Christmas now.

Here Comes Santa Claus
(Right Down Santa Claus Lane)

Words and Music by Gene Autry and Oakley Haldeman

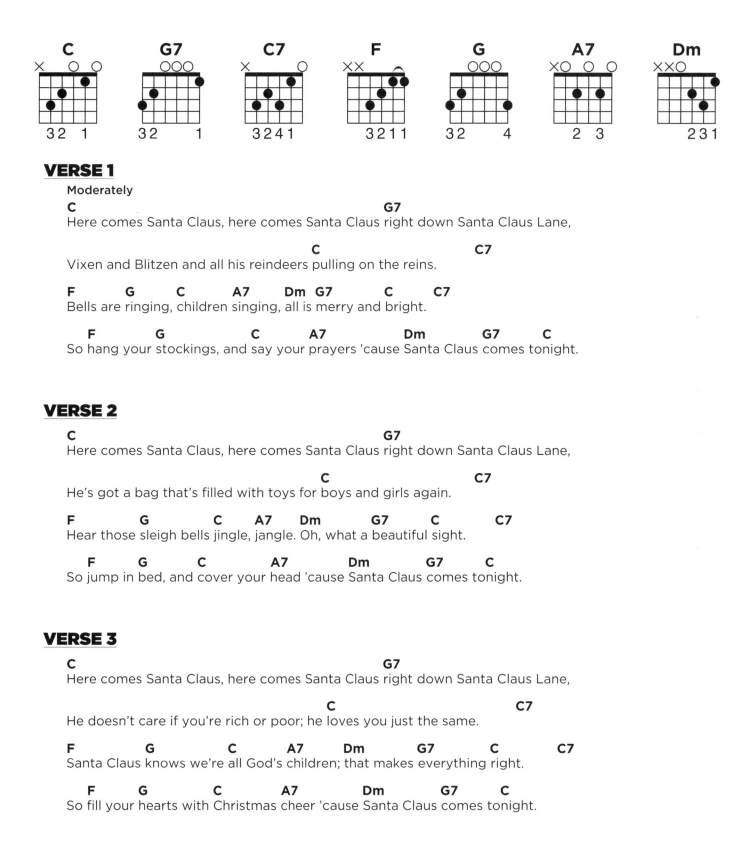

VERSE 1

Moderately

C   G7
Here comes Santa Claus, here comes Santa Claus right down Santa Claus Lane,

             C   C7
Vixen and Blitzen and all his reindeers pulling on the reins.

F   G   C   A7 Dm G7   C   C7
Bells are ringing, children singing, all is merry and bright.

  F   G   C   A7   Dm   G7   C
So hang your stockings, and say your prayers 'cause Santa Claus comes tonight.

VERSE 2

C   G7
Here comes Santa Claus, here comes Santa Claus right down Santa Claus Lane,

             C   C7
He's got a bag that's filled with toys for boys and girls again.

F   G   C A7 Dm   G7   C   C7
Hear those sleigh bells jingle, jangle. Oh, what a beautiful sight.

  F   G   C   A7   Dm   G7   C
So jump in bed, and cover your head 'cause Santa Claus comes tonight.

VERSE 3

C   G7
Here comes Santa Claus, here comes Santa Claus right down Santa Claus Lane,

             C   C7
He doesn't care if you're rich or poor; he loves you just the same.

F   G   C A7 Dm   G7   C   C7
Santa Claus knows we're all God's children; that makes everything right.

  F   G   C   A7   Dm   G7   C
So fill your hearts with Christmas cheer 'cause Santa Claus comes tonight.

VERSE 4

C   G7
Here comes Santa Claus, here comes Santa Claus right down Santa Claus Lane,

                   C   C7
He'll come around when chimes ring out that it's Christmas morn again.

F   G   C   A7 Dm G7   C   C7
Peace on earth will come to all if we just follow the light.

  F   G   C A7   Dm   G7   C
So let's give thanks to the Lord above 'cause Santa Claus comes tonight.

REPEAT VERSE 1

Jingle Bell Rock

Words and Music by Joe Beal and Jim Boothe

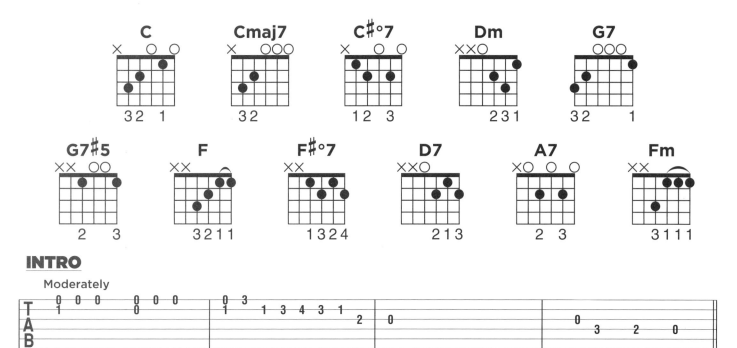

INTRO

Moderately

VERSE 1

C   Cmaj7   C   C#°7   Dm   G7
Jingle bell, jingle bell, jingle bell rock, jingle bells swing, and jingle bells ring.

Dm   G7   Dm   G7 Dm   G7#5
Snowin' and blowin' up bushels of fun;   now the jingle hop has begun.

VERSE 2

C   Cmaj7   C   C#°7   Dm   G7
Jingle bell, jingle bell, jingle bell rock, jingle bells chime in jingle bell time.

Dm   G7   Dm   G7 Dm   G7   C
Dancin' and prancin' in Jingle Bell Square   in the frosty air.

BRIDGE

F   F#°7   C
What a bright time, it's the right time to rock the night away.

D7   G7
Jingle bell time is a swell time   to go glidin' in a one-horse sleigh.

VERSE 3

C   Cmaj7   C   A7
Giddy-yap, jingle horse, pick up your feet. Jingle around the clock.

F   Fm   D7   G7   C
Mix and mingle in a jinglin' beat,   that's the jingle bell rock.

REPEAT VERSE 2

REPEAT BRIDGE

VERSE 4

C   Cmaj7   C   A7
Giddy-yap, jingle horse, pick up your feet. Jingle around the clock.

F   Fm   D7   G7   D7   G7
Mix and mingle in a jinglin' beat,   that's the jingle bell,   that's the jingle bell,

D7   G7   C
that's the jingle bell rock.

Let It Snow! Let It Snow! Let It Snow!

Words by Sammy Cahn
Music by Jule Styne

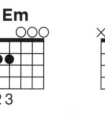

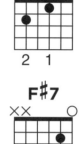

D   A7   A   E7   Em   B7   Bm7   F#7

VERSE 1

Moderately

        D   A7   D   A   E7   A
Oh, the weather outside is frightful, but the fire is so delightful,

   Em   B7   Em   A7   D
and since we've no place to go, let it snow, let it snow, let it snow!

VERSE 2

       D   A7   D   A   E7   A
It doesn't show signs of stopping, and I brought some corn for popping.

   Em   B7   Em   A7   D
The lights are turned way down low. Let it snow, let it snow, let it snow!

BRIDGE

          A   Bm7   E7   A
When we finally kiss goodnight, how I'll hate going out in the storm.

               F#7   B7   E7   A   A7
But if you really hold me tight, all the way home I'll be warm.

VERSE 3

       D   A7   D   A   E7   A
The fire is slowly dying, and, my dear, we're still goodbye-ing,

   Em   B7   Em   A7   D
but as long as you love me so, let it snow, let it snow, let it snow!

Silver Bells

from the Paramount Picture THE LEMON DROP KID
Words and Music by Jay Livingston and Ray Evans

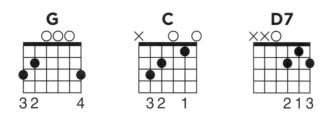

CHORUS

Moderately

G   C   D7   G
Silver bells, silver bells, it's Christmas time in the city.

     C   D7   G
Ring-a-ling, hear them ring, soon it will be Christmas Day.

VERSE 1

    G   C
City sidewalks, busy sidewalks dressed in holiday style;

    D7   G
in the air, there's a feeling of Christmas.

                   C
Children laughing, people passing, meeting smile after smile,

    D7   G   D7
and on every street corner you hear:

REPEAT CHORUS

VERSE 2

    G   C
Strings of street lights, even stoplights blink a bright red and green

  D7   G
as the shoppers rush home with their treasures.

                  C
Hear the snow crunch, see the kids bunch, this is Santa's big scene,

  D7   G   D7
and above all this bustle you hear:

REPEAT CHORUS

The Little Drummer Boy

Words and Music by Harry Simeone, Henry Onorati and Katherine Davis

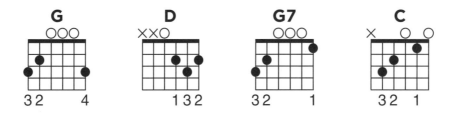

VERSE 1

Slowly

G
Come, they told me, pa, rum, pum, pum, pum,

a newborn King to see, pa, rum, pum, pum, pum.

D
    Our finest gifts we bring, pa, rum, pum, pum, pum,

    G   **G7**   **C**   **G**   **D**
to lay before the King, pa, rum, pum, pum, pum, rum, pum, pum, pum, rum pum, pum, pum.

G
So to honor Him, pa, rum, pum, pum, pum, when we come.

VERSE 2

G
Baby Jesus, pa, rum, pum, pum, pum,

I am a poor boy too, pa, rum, pum, pum, pum.

D
    I have no gift to bring, pa, rum, pum, pum, pum,

    G   **G7**   **C**   **G**   **D**
that's fit to give our King, pa, rum, pum, pum, pum, rum, pum, pum, pum, rum pum, pum, pum.

G
Shall I play for you, pa, rum, pum, pum, pum, on my drum?

VERSE 3

G
Mary nodded, pa, rum, pum, pum, pum.

The ox and lamb kept time, pa, rum, pum, pum, pum.

D
   I played my drum for him, pa, rum, pum, pum, pum.

           G   **G7**   **C**   **G**   **D**
I played my best for him, pa, rum, pum, pum, pum, rum, pum, pum, pum, rum pum, pum, pum.

G
Then He smiled at me, pa, rum, pum, pum, pum, on my drum.

Mary, Did You Know?

Words and Music by Mark Lowry and Buddy Greene

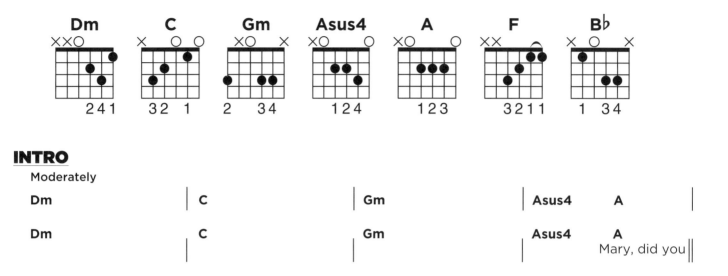

INTRO

Moderately

Dm		C		Gm		Asus4	A	

Dm		C		Gm		Asus4	A	

Mary, did you

VERSE 1

Dm   C   Gm   Asus4
know that your baby boy would one day walk on water?

A   Dm   C   Gm   Asus4
Mary, did you know that your baby boy would save our sons and daughters?

A   Gm   C   F   C   Dm
   Did you know that your baby boy has come to make you new?

Gm   Asus4   A
This child that you delivered will soon deliver you.

VERSE 2

Dm   C   Gm   Asus4
Mary, did you know that your baby boy will give sight to a blind man?

A   Dm   C   Gm   Asus4
Mary, did you know that your baby boy would calm a storm with His hand?

A   Gm   C   F   C   Dm
   Did you know that your baby boy has walked where angels trod,

Gm   Asus4   A
and when you kissed your little baby, you've kissed the face of God? Oh, Mary, did you

INTERLUDE

Dm	**C**	**Gm**	**Asus4**	**A**
know?				Mary, did you

Dm	**C**	**Gm**	**Asus4**	**A**
know?				The

BRIDGE

Bb   **C**   **Dm**   **C**   **Bb**
blind will see, the deaf will hear, the dead will live again,

   Gm   **C**   **Dm**   **Asus4**   **A**
the lame will leap, the dumb will speak the praises of the Lamb.

VERSE 3

       Dm   **C**   **Gm**   **Asus4**
Mary, did you know that your baby boy is Lord of all creation?

A   **Dm**   **C**   **Gm**   **Asus4**
Mary, did you know that your baby boy will one day rule the nations?

A   **Gm**   **C**   **F**   **C**   **Dm**
     Did you know that your baby boy was heaven's perfect Lamb,

   Gm   **Asus4**   **A**
and the sleeping Child you're holding is the great   I

OUTRO

Dm	**C**	**Gm**	**Asus4**	**A**	**Dm**
Am?					

C	**Gm**	**Asus4**	**A**	**Dm**

Merry Christmas, Darling

Words and Music by Richard Carpenter and Frank Pooler

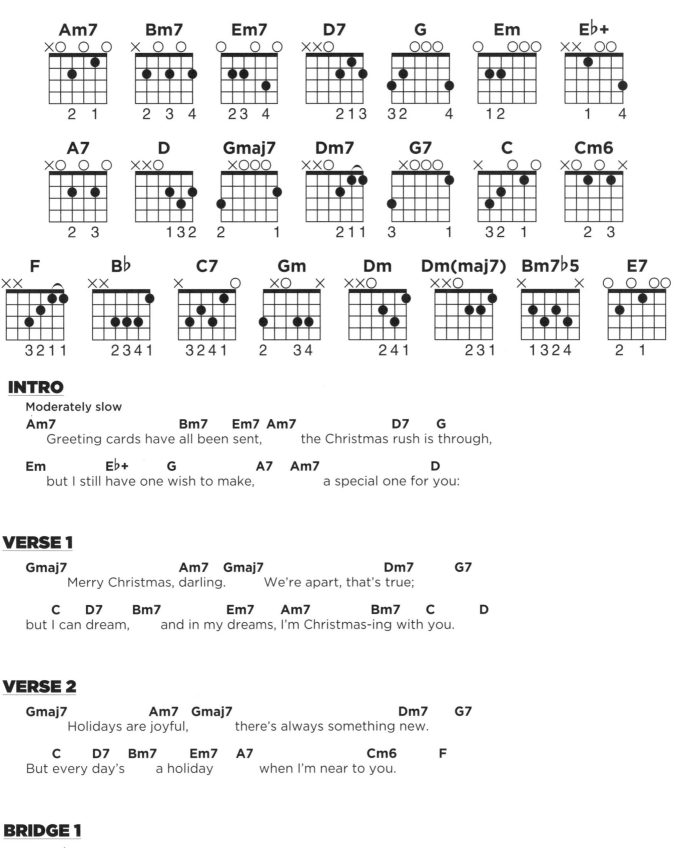

INTRO

Moderately slow

| Am7 | | Bm7 | Em7 | Am7 | | D7 | G |
Greeting cards have all been sent,   the Christmas rush is through,

| Em | | Eb+ | G | | A7 | Am7 | | D |
but I still have one wish to make,   a special one for you:

VERSE 1

| Gmaj7 | | Am7 | Gmaj7 | | Dm7 | G7 |
Merry Christmas, darling.   We're apart, that's true;

| C | D7 | Bm7 | | Em7 | Am7 | | Bm7 | C | | D |
but I can dream,   and in my dreams, I'm Christmas-ing with you.

VERSE 2

| Gmaj7 | | Am7 | Gmaj7 | | Dm7 | G7 |
Holidays are joyful,   there's always something new.

| C | D7 | Bm7 | | Em7 | A7 | | Cm6 | F |
But every day's   a holiday   when I'm near to you.

BRIDGE 1

| Bb | | C7 | Am7 | | Dm7 | Gm | | C | F | C |
The lights on my tree I wish you could see,   I wish it every day.

| Dm | | Dm(maj7) | Dm7 | | D7 | G | | Am7 | Bm7 | Am7 | D7 |
The logs on the fire   fill me with desire   to see you and to say   that I

VERSE 3

Gmaj7   Am7 Gmaj7   Dm7 G7
wish you merry Christmas, happy New Year too.

  C   D7   Bm7   Em7   Am7
I've just one wish on this Christmas Eve: (On this Christmas Eve.)

   D7   G
I wish I were with you.

BRIDGE 2

B♭   C7 |Am7   Dm7 |Gm   C |F   C

  Dm   Dm(maj7) Dm7   D7 G   Am7 Bm7 Am7 D7
The logs on the fire fill me with desire to see you and to say   that I

VERSE 4

Gmaj7   Am7 Gmaj7   Dm7 G7
wish you merry Christmas, happy New Year too.

  C   D7   Bm7   Em7   Am7
I've just one wish on this Christmas Eve: (On this Christmas Eve.)

  D7   Bm7♭5 E7   Am7   D7   G
I wish I were with you.   I wish I were with you.

My Favorite Things

from THE SOUND OF MUSIC

Lyrics by Oscar Hammerstein II
Music by Richard Rodgers

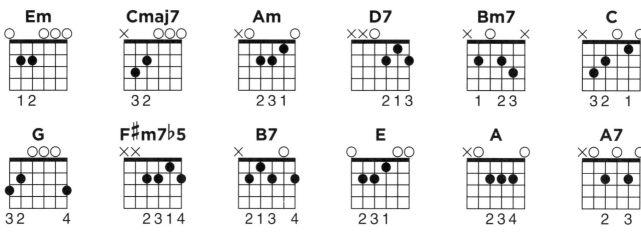

INTRO

Moderately

VERSE 1

Em
Raindrops on roses and whiskers on kittens,

Cmaj7
bright copper kettles and warm woolen mittens,

Am　　　　**D7**　　**Bm7**　　　**C**
brown paper packages tied up with strings,

G　　　**C**　　　**F♯m7♭5**　**B7**　　　　**Em**
these are a few of my favorite　things.

VERSE 2

Em
Cream-colored ponies and crisp apple strudels,

Cmaj7
doorbells and sleighbells and schnitzel with noodles,

Am　　　　**D7**　　**Bm7**　　　**C**
wild geese that fly with the moon on their wings,

G　　　**C**　　　**F♯m7♭5**　**B7**　　　　　**E**
these are a few of my favorite　things.

VERSE 3

E
Girls in white dresses with blue satin sashes,

A
snowflakes that stay on my nose and eyelashes,

Am   **D7**   **Bm7**   **C**
silver white winters that melt into springs,

G   **C**   **F♯m7♭5** **B7**
these are a few of my favorite   things.

BRIDGE 1

Em   **F♯m7♭5**   **B7**   **Em**   **C**
When the dog bites,   when the bee stings,   when I'm feeling sad,

              A7   **G**   **C** **D7** **G**   **F♯m7♭5**   **B7**
I simply remember my favorite things, and then I don't feel   so bad.

REPEAT VERSE 1

REPEAT VERSE 2

REPEAT VERSE 3

BRIDGE 2

Em   **F♯m7♭5**   **B7**   **Em**   **C**
When the dog bites,   when the bee stings,   when I'm feeling sad,

              A7   **G**   **C** **D7** **G**
I simply remember my favorite things, and then I don't feel   so bad.

Rudolph the Red-Nosed Reindeer

Music and Lyrics by Johnny Marks

 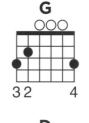 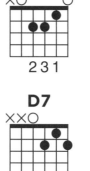 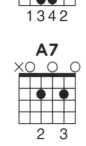 

C   Bm   Am   G

Em   A7   D7   D

INTRO

Freely

              C   Bm   Am   G
You know Dasher and Dancer and Prancer and Vixen,

C   Bm   Am   G
Comet and Cupid and Donner and Blitzen,

Em   A7   D7
but do you recall the most famous reindeer of all?

VERSE 1

Moderately fast

G   D7
Rudolph the red-nosed reindeer had a very shiny nose,

                             G
and if you ever saw it, you would even say it glows.

                              D7
All of the other reindeer used to laugh and call him names.

                              G
They never let poor Rudolph join in any reindeer games.

BRIDGE

C   G   D7   G
Then one foggy Christmas Eve, Santa came to say,

D   Em   A7   D7
"Rudolph, with your nose so bright, won't you guide my sleigh tonight?"

VERSE 2

G   D7
Then how the reindeer loved him, as they shouted out with glee:

                                                                    G
"Rudolph the red-nosed reindeer, you'll go down in history!"

REPEAT VERSE 1

REPEAT BRIDGE

REPEAT VERSE 2

Santa Claus Is Comin' to Town

Words by Haven Gillespie
Music by J. Fred Coots

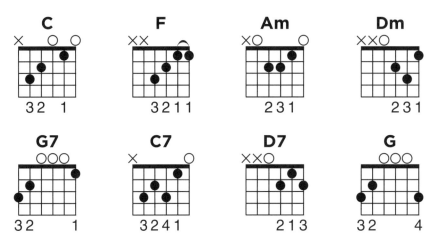

VERSE 1

Moderately

     C   F   C   F
You better watch out, you better not cry, better not pout, I'm telling you why:

C   Am   Dm   G7   C   G7
Santa Claus is comin'   to town.

VERSE 2

     C   F   C   F
He's making a list and checking it twice, gonna find out who's naughty and nice.

C   Am   Dm   G7   C
Santa Claus is comin'   to town.

BRIDGE 1

    C7   F   C7   F
He sees you when you're sleeping. He knows when you're awake.

    D7   G   D7   G7
He knows if you've been bad or good, so be good for goodness sake.

VERSE 3

       C   F   C   F
Oh! You better watch out, you better not cry, better not pout, I'm telling you why:

C   Am   Dm   G7   C
Santa Claus is comin'   to town.

VERSE 4

      C   F   C   F

With little tin horns and little toy drums, rooty toot toots and rummy tum tums.

C   Am   Dm   G7   C   G7

Santa Claus is comin'   to town.

VERSE 5

      C   F   C   F

With curly head dolls that cuddle and coo, elephants, boats and kiddy cars, too.

C   Am   Dm   G7   C

Santa Claus is comin'   to town.

BRIDGE 2

      C7   F   C7   F

The kids in girl and boyland will have a jubilee.

      D7   G   D7   G7

They're gonna build a toyland town all around the Christmas tree.

REPEAT VERSE 3

Sleigh Ride

Music by Leroy Anderson
Words by Mitchell Parish

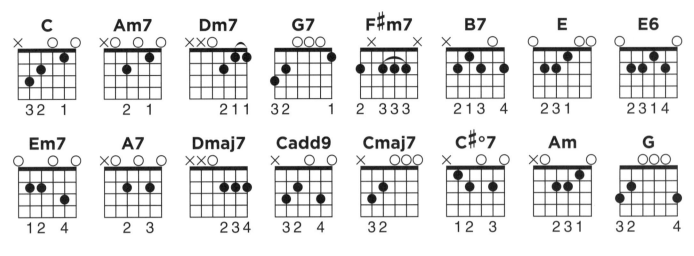

VERSE 1

Moderately

N.C.   **C**   **Am7**   **Dm7**   **G7**   **C**   **Am7**   **Dm7**
Just hear those sleigh bells jingling, ring-ting-tingling too.

    G7   **C**   **Am7**   **Dm7**   **G7**   **C**   **Am7**   **Dm7**
Come on, it's lovely weather for a sleigh ride together with you.

    G7   **C**   **Am7**   **Dm7**   **G7**   **C**   **Am7**   **Dm7**
Outside the snow is falling and friends are calling, "Yoo hoo."

    G7   **C**   **Am7**   **Dm7**   **G7**   **C**
Come on, it's lovely weather for a sleigh ride together with you.

BRIDGE 1

    F♯m7   **B7**   **E**   **E6**
Giddy-yap, giddy-yap, giddy-yap, let's go,   let's look at the show.

F♯m7   **B7**   **E**
    We're riding in a wonderland of snow.

    Em7   **A7**   **Dmaj7**
Giddy-yap, giddy-yap, giddy-yap, it's grand   just holding your hand.

Dm7   **G7**   **Dm7**   **G7**
    We're gliding along with a song of a wintery fairy - land.

VERSE 2

```
N.C.            C       Am7   Dm7   G7        C         Am7       Dm7
Our cheeks are nice and rosy and comfy, cozy are we.

        G7      C       Am7       Dm7     G7          C         Am7       Dm7
We've snuggled close together like two birds of a feather would be.

        G7      C       Am7       Dm7   G7        C         Am7       Dm7
Let's take that road before us and sing a chorus or two.

        G7      C     Am7       Dm7        G7          C
Come on, it's lovely weather for a sleigh ride together with you.
```

BRIDGE 2

```
N.C.    Cadd9                           Cmaj7
There's a birthday party at the home of farmer Gray.

                                        C
It'll be the perfect ending of a perfect day.

        C#°7                 Dm7   B7      C    E    Am
We'll be singing the songs we love to sing without a single stop

        E                   B7              E    G
at the fireplace where we'll watch the chestnuts pop.    Pop, pop, pop!

        Cadd9                           Cmaj7
There's a happy feeling nothing in the world can buy

                                        C
when they pass around the coffee and the pumpkin pie.

    C#°7            Dm7   B7      C    E    Am
It'll nearly be like a picture print by Currier and Ives.

Dm7                                         G7
    These wonderful things are the things we remember all through our lives.
```

REPEAT VERSE 1

OUTRO (REPEAT AND FADE)

```
 ||: C       Am7       | Dm7       G7       | C       Am7       | Dm7       G7       :||
     you.               |                    | Lovely    weather for a | sleigh ride together with
```

Winter Wonderland

Words by Dick Smith
Music by Felix Bernard

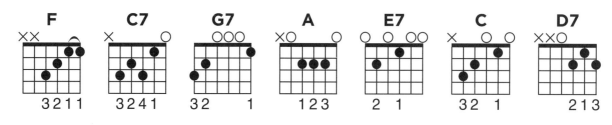

VERSE 1

Moderately

       F   C7
Sleigh bells ring, are you listenin'? In the lane, snow is glistenin'.

                              G7   C7   F
A beautiful sight, we're happy tonight walkin' in a winter wonderland.

VERSE 2

       F   C7
Gone away is the bluebird. Here to stay is a new bird.

                              G7   C7   F
He sings a love song as we go along walkin' in a winter wonderland.

BRIDGE 1

A   E7   A   E7   A
In the meadow, we can build a snowman and pretend that he is Parson Brown.

C   G7   C   D7   G7   C   C7
He'll say, "Are you married?" We'll say, "No, man! But you can do the job when you're in town!"

VERSE 3

       F   C7
Later on we'll conspire, as we dream by the fire,

                              G7   C7   F
to face unafraid the plans that we've made walkin' in a winter wonderland.

REPEAT VERSE 1

REPEAT VERSE 2

BRIDGE 2

A   E7   A   E7   A

In the meadow, we can build a snowman and pretend that he's a circus clown.

C   G7   C   D7   G7   C   C7

We'll have lots of fun with mister snowman until the other kiddies knock him down!

REPEAT VERSE 3

White Christmas

from the Motion Picture Irving Berlin's HOLIDAY INN
Words and Music by Irving Berlin

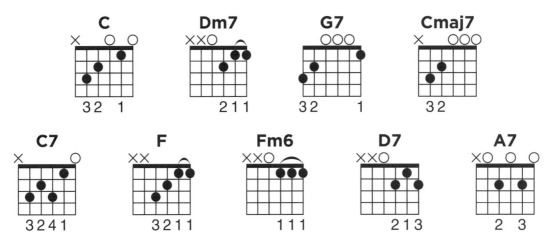

VERSE 1

Moderately slow

```
C              Dm7  G7   Dm7          G7        Cmaj7
I'm dreaming of a white Christmas,     just like the ones I used to know,

G7          C  Cmaj7 C7      F    Fm6   C          D7  Dm7        G7
   where the treetops    glisten and children listen to hear sleigh bells in the snow.

C              Dm7  G7   Dm7          G7        Cmaj7
I'm dreaming of a white Christmas,     with every Christmas card I write:

G7          C  Cmaj7 C7     F    Fm6    C  A7  Dm7    G7  C       G7
   "May your days be    merry and bright     and may all  your Christmases be white."
```

VERSE 2

```
C              Dm7  G7   Dm7          G7        Cmaj7
I'm dreaming of a white Christmas,     just like the ones I used to know,

G7          C  Cmaj7 C7      F    Fm6   C          D7  Dm7        G7
   where the treetops    glisten and children listen to hear sleigh bells in the snow.

C              Dm7  G7   Dm7          G7        Cmaj7
I'm dreaming of a white Christmas,     with every Christmas card I write:

G7          C  Cmaj7 C7     F    Fm6    C  A7  Dm7    G7  C
   "May your days be    merry and bright     and may all  your Christmases be white."
```

GUITAR NOTATION LEGEND

Chord Diagrams

CHORD DIAGRAMS graphically represent the guitar fretboard to show correct chord fingerings.
- The letter above the diagram tells the name of the chord.
- The top, bold horizontal line represents the nut of the guitar. Each thin horizontal line represents a fret. Each vertical line represents a string; the low E string is on the far left and the high E string is on the far right.
- A dot shows where to put your fret-hand finger and the number at the bottom of the diagram tells which finger to use.
- The "O" above the string means play it open, while an "X" means don't play the string.

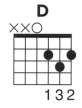

Tablature

TABLATURE graphically represents the guitar fingerboard. Each horizontal line represents a string, and each number represents a fret.

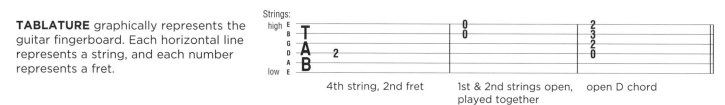

4th string, 2nd fret   1st & 2nd strings open, played together   open D chord

Definitions for Special Guitar Notation

HAMMER-ON: Strike the first (lower) note with one finger, then sound the higher note (on the same string) with another finger by fretting it without picking.

PULL-OFF: Place both fingers on the notes to be sounded. Strike the first note and without picking, pull the finger off to sound the second (lower) note.

LEGATO SLIDE: Strike the first note and then slide the same fret-hand finger up or down to the second note. The second note is not struck.

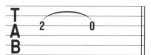

SHIFT SLIDE: Same as legato slide, except the second note is struck.

Additional Musical Definitions

N.C.   • No chord. Instrument is silent.

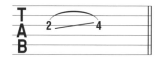

• Repeat measures between signs.

Guitar Chord Songbooks

Each 6" x 9" book includes complete lyrics, chord symbols, and guitar chord diagrams.

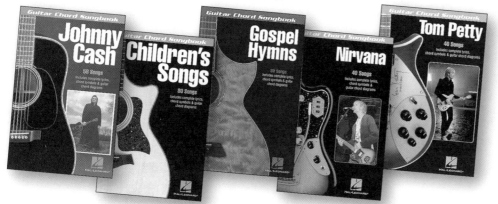

Acoustic Hits
00701787 . . . . $14.99

Acoustic Rock
00699540 . . . . $21.99

Alabama
00699914 . . . . $14.95

The Beach Boys
00699566 . . . . $19.99

The Beatles
00699562 . . . . $17.99

Bluegrass
00702585 . . . . $14.99

Johnny Cash
00699648 . . . . $17.99

Children's Songs
00699539 . . . . $16.99

Christmas Carols
00699536 . . . . $12.99

Christmas Songs
00119911 . . . . $14.99

Eric Clapton
00699567 . . . . $19.99

Classic Rock
00699598 . . . . $18.99

Coffeehouse Hits
00703318 . . . . $14.99

Country
00699534 . . . . $17.99

Country Favorites
00700609 . . . . $14.99

Country Hits
00140859 . . . . $14.99

Country Standards
00700608 . . . . $12.95

Cowboy Songs
00699636 . . . . $19.99

Creedence Clearwater Revival
00701786 . . . . $16.99

Jim Croce
00148087 . . . . $14.99

Crosby, Stills & Nash
00701609 . . . . $16.99

John Denver
02501697 . . . . $17.99

Neil Diamond
00700606 . . . . $19.99

Disney – 2nd Edition
00295786 . . . . $17.99

The Doors
00699888 . . . . $17.99

Eagles
00122917 . . . . $17.99

Early Rock
00699916 . . . . $14.99

Folksongs
00699541 . . . . $14.99

Folk Pop Rock
00699651 . . . . $17.99

40 Easy Strumming Songs
00115972 . . . . $16.99

Four Chord Songs
00701611 . . . . $14.99

Glee
00702501 . . . . $14.99

Gospel Hymns
00700463 . . . . $14.99

Grand Ole Opry®
00699885 . . . . $16.95

Grateful Dead
00139461 . . . . $14.99

Green Day
00103074 . . . . $14.99

Irish Songs
00701044 . . . . $14.99

Michael Jackson
00137847 . . . . $14.99

Billy Joel
00699632 . . . . $19.99

Elton John
00699732 . . . . $15.99

Ray LaMontagne
00130337 . . . . $12.99

Latin Songs
00700973 . . . . $14.99

Love Songs
00701043 . . . . $14.99

Bob Marley
00701704 . . . . $17.99

Bruno Mars
00125332 . . . . $12.99

Paul McCartney
00385035 . . . . $16.95

Steve Miller
00701146 . . . . $12.99

Modern Worship
00701801 . . . . $16.99

Motown
00699734 . . . . $17.99

Willie Nelson
00148273 . . . . $17.99

Nirvana
00699762 . . . . $16.99

Roy Orbison
00699752 . . . . $17.99

Peter, Paul & Mary
00103013 . . . . $19.99

Tom Petty
00699883 . . . . $15.99

Pink Floyd
00139116 . . . . $14.99

Pop/Rock
00699538 . . . . $16.99

Praise & Worship
00699634 . . . . $14.99

Elvis Presley
00699633 . . . . $17.99

Queen
00702395 . . . . $14.99

Red Hot Chili Peppers
00699710 . . . . $19.99

The Rolling Stones
00137716 . . . . $17.99

Bob Seger
00701147 . . . . $12.99

Carly Simon
00121011 . . . . $14.99

Sting
00699921 . . . . $17.99

Taylor Swift
00263755 . . . . $16.99

Three Chord Acoustic Songs
00123860 . . . . $14.99

Three Chord Songs
00699720 . . . . $17.99

Two-Chord Songs
00119236 . . . . $16.99

U2
00137744 . . . . $14.99

Hank Williams
00700607 . . . . $16.99

Stevie Wonder
00120862 . . . . $14.99

Prices and availability subject to change without notice.

HAL•LEONARD®
Visit Hal Leonard online at **www.halleonard.com**

1120
9/12; 480